BBC earth

DO YOU KNOW?

Level 3

REPTILES

Inspired by BBC Earth TV series and developed with
input from BBC Earth natural history specialists

Written by Alex Woolf
Text adapted by Carrie Lewis
Series Editor: Nick Coates

LADYBIRD BOOKS

UK | USA | Canada | Ireland | Australia
India | New Zealand | South Africa

Ladybird Books is part of the Penguin Random House group of companies
whose addresses can be found at global.penguinrandomhouse.com.
www.penguin.co.uk   www.puffin.co.uk   www.ladybird.co.uk

First published 2020
001

Printed in China

A CIP catalogue record for this book is available from the British Library

ISBN: 978-0-241-38288-2

All correspondence to:
Ladybird Books Ltd
Penguin Random House Children's
One Embassy Gardens, New Union Square,
5 Nine Elms Lane, London SW8 5DA

Contents

New words

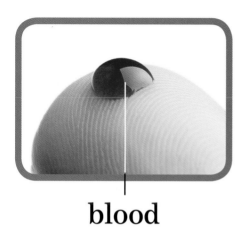

blood

breathe

desert

glide

hunt
(verb)

land
(noun)

lay eggs

nest

predator

prey
(noun)

rainforest

venom

What are reptiles?

Reptiles live in most parts of the Earth.

Some reptiles live on **land** and some live in the water. But all reptiles **breathe** out of the water.

Lizards, snakes, turtles, tortoises and crocodiles are all reptiles.

scale

Most reptiles have scales on their bodies.

shell

Some reptiles, like turtles, have a shell.

Some reptiles eat other animals.

Some reptiles eat grass and plants.

THINK!

Some reptiles have scales and live in the sea, but they are not fish. How are reptiles different to fish?

How do reptiles stay warm?

Many animals have warm **blood**. This helps them to stay warm.

Reptiles have cold blood. They sit in the sun to get warm.

Reptiles do not move a lot when it is cold.

This Komodo dragon has a big body, which helps it to stay warm.

The nose-horned chameleon is very small. It gets cold quickly.

FIND OUT!

Use books or the internet to find out which other animals have cold blood.

Do all reptiles lay eggs?

A few reptiles do not **lay eggs**. They have babies. But most reptiles lay eggs.

Most reptiles do not stay with their eggs or babies.

Sea turtles lay eggs in a **nest** on the beach. The mother does not stay with her eggs.

Some snakes, crocodiles and tortoises lay eggs.

Crocodiles stay with their babies to keep them safe from **predators**.

 WATCH!

Watch the video (see page 32).
How many sea turtles can come to the island in one night?

How do reptiles live in the desert?

It is hot in the **desert** and there isn't much water.

Many reptiles stay under the sand in the day.

They find food at night when it isn't hot.

This desert tortoise lives under the sand, where it isn't hot.

The rattlesnake moves quickly because the sand is very hot.

water

The gecko gets water from its skin and eyes.

PROJECT

Work in a group.

Find out as much as you can about the desert tortoise. Make a chart showing what it eats, where it lives, what its predators are and other interesting facts. Stick on a picture of the tortoise.

Which reptiles live in rainforests?

Many reptiles live in **rainforests**.

Some reptiles live in rivers.
Some live in trees.

This caiman is waiting in a river. It catches small animals when they come near.

This white-lipped pit viper waits in trees for its **prey**.

tongue

The Parson's chameleon does not move when it **hunts**. Only its eyes move. Then it catches prey with its long tongue.

LOOK!

Look at the pages.
Which parts of the chameleon's body move when it hunts?

Which reptiles live in water?

Lots of reptiles live in water. Some reptiles live in rivers and some live in seas.

Sea turtles live at sea most of the time. They only come to the land to lay their eggs.

Sea snakes live in the sea, but they put their heads out of the water to breathe.

This marine iguana is looking for food in the water.

Marine iguanas get cold in the water. They sit in the sun to get warm again.

LOOK!

Look at the pages.
Where do sea turtles go to lay their eggs?

How do reptiles stay safe?

Reptiles have many predators.

It is hard to stay safe.
Lizards run very fast to stay safe.

Some lizards lose their tails when a predator catches them, but they can grow a new tail.

tail

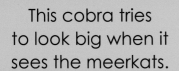
This cobra tries to look big when it sees the meerkats.

This gecko is light brown. Predators cannot see it on the sand.

The gecko is green and brown. It is hard to see it on a tree.

gecko

 WATCH!

Watch the video (see page 32).
Why do the iguanas need to run past the snakes?
Where do the snakes live?

What do snakes eat?

Most snakes eat small animals and eggs.
They eat lizards, birds, fish and other snakes.

This green mamba snake kills its prey with **venom**.

Some snakes eat very big animals. Snakes can eat these big animals because they have big mouths.

Big snakes can eat big animals!

This python uses its long body to hold its prey. The prey can't breathe.

LOOK!

Look at the pages.
How can snakes swallow big animals?

What cleans a turtle?

Green sea turtles travel a long way across the seas.

Very small animals, called parasites, live on the turtles. The turtles don't like them because the parasites can hurt or kill the turtles.

The turtles swim to a place where there are cleaner fish. The cleaner fish eat the parasites on the turtles' shells.

A lot of turtles wait for the cleaner fish to clean their shells.

THINK!

Why do the fish clean the turtles?

Can reptiles fly?

Reptiles cannot fly like birds. But some of them can **glide**.

The little Draco lizard lives in the trees.

It can change its body to make wings. Then it can glide from tree to tree.

The flying snake glides from tree to tree. The snake changes its body to help it glide.

▶ **WATCH!**

Watch the video (see page 32).
Why does the Draco lizard jump from the tree?
How far can a Draco lizard glide?

How do crocodiles hunt?

Crocodiles hunt their prey in water. Only their eyes and noses stay above the water. They wait for prey to come near.

Crocodiles have very good eyes and ears. They can feel when things move in the water, too.

This crocodile sees its prey and jumps out of the water.

It catches its prey and pulls it under the water.

THINK!

Why do crocodiles hide their bodies under the water when they hunt?

What are the biggest and smallest reptiles?

There are many different reptiles.
Some reptiles are big and some are small.
Some reptiles are long and some are short.

The Burmese python can be longer than three people.

The saltwater crocodile is the biggest and heaviest reptile on Earth.

Some reptiles are very small. The dwarf gecko is smaller than the end of a finger!

FIND OUT!

What is the biggest sea turtle in the world?
Use books or the internet to find out.

Quiz

Choose the correct answers.

1 Which sentence is NOT true?
  a All reptiles breathe out of the water.
  b Most reptiles have scales.
  c No reptiles have shells.

2 Reptiles have . . .
  a warm blood.
  b cold blood.
  c no blood.

3 Which sentence is true?
  a No reptiles lay eggs.
  b Most reptiles lay eggs.
  c All reptiles lay eggs.

4 Why do desert reptiles stay under the sand in the day?
  a It is hot in the day.
  b There is no food in the day.
  c There is no water in the day.

5 Which sentence is true?
   a No reptiles live in water.
   b Lots of reptiles live in water.
   c All reptiles live in water.

6 Why do sea turtles come to the land?
   a to breathe
   b to lay eggs
   c to eat

7 The green mamba snake
   kills its prey with . . .
   a its eyes.
   b its nose.
   c its venom.

8 What eats the parasites on
   green sea turtles?
   a cleaner fish
   b other parasites
   c other turtles

Visit **www.ladybirdeducation.co.uk** for
FREE DO YOU KNOW? teaching resources.

- video clips with simplified voiceover and subtitles
- video and comprehension activities
- class projects and lesson plans
- audio recording of every book
- digital version of every book
- full answer keys

To access video clips, audio tracks and digital books:

1 Go to **www.ladybirdeducation.co.uk**
2 Click "Unlock book"
3 Enter the code below

2DBiyaeUC0

Stay safe online! Some of the DO YOU KNOW? activities ask children to do extra research online. Remember:

- ensure an adult is supervising;
- use established search engines such as Google or Kiddle;
- children should never share personal details, such as name, home or school address, telephone number or photos.